Browns Guide

Boutique Hotels
UK

ISBN-13: 978-1478367062

Foreword

Within this guide we have attempted to bring you the very best of the current contemporary, boutique and luxury hotels available within the UK today.

We have listed our choice by area, and not always cost defined, although it normally goes without saying, that this level of accommodation does come with a price tag. That said, we have found some surprisingly good quality for value places.

The guide comes with postcode reference and web-links for your total convenience. We are always interested in adding to our list, so if you have a special place that you think we should look at – please let us know. And we will check it out for inclusion in our next update – contact details can be found at the rear of the guide.

For those looking for the most prestigious names rather than the more unusual or designer lead hotels, there's a separate section to the rear of this guide.

I hope you find this guide of use, and more importantly, I hope you enjoy the hotel of your choice.

Carolyn Brown

Editor

Counties

6   Avon
11 Bedfordshire
10 Berkshire
15 Cambridgeshire
18 Cheshire
21 Cornwall
39 Cumbria
42 Devon
49 Dorset
51 East Anglia
52 Essex
53 Gloucestershire
60 Gt Manchester
65 Hampshire
69 Herefordshire
70 Isle of Wight
72 Kent
76 Lancashire
87 London
102 Merseyside
103 Oxfordshire
105 Scotland
112 Somerset
117 Suffolk
118 Surrey

Cont'd

119 Sussex
124 Wales
132 Warwickshire & West Midlands
133 Wirral
135 Worcestershire
136 Yorkshire

Avon

Thirty Eight - 38 Upper Belgrave Road, Clifton
Bristol -BS8-2XN

One look at their website will tell you that this
boutique hotel is something really special. From the
Décor to the dressing gowns, the visitor is catered for.
They offer ten stylish bedrooms in a recently
refurbished Georgian merchant's house at the top of
the City – Simply First-Class

Ideal for the many shops, bars and restaurants that
Clifton has to offer.

NB they do not cater for children under 12 years of
age.

Tel: 44(0)1179 466 905
web: www.number38clifton.com

Tariff – POA

The Bristol Hotel - Prince Street, Bristol BS1-4QF

The perfect location - sitting on the quayside of the Floating Harbour, this rather special hotel is surrounded by the best of Bristol's Old City and maritime history - check out rates for a deal
With ultra cool bars and public areas, it's easy to forget you are actually in an English city, so continental is the feel.

The bedrooms are clean-lined and stylish, so if modern is your taste, and unusual setting are what you seek, this could be the hotel for you.

Tel: 44 (0)117 923 0333
web: www.doylecollection.com
Rates –POA

NB -The hotel does not have it's own car park. However, there is an NCP car park immediately adjacent to the hotel with direct hotel access.

The Queensberry Hotel - Russell Street, Bath - BA1 2QF

The Queensberry Hotel, is certainly one of the most beautiful hotels in Bath. Run by the husband and wife team - Laurence & Helen Beere - the place has a very unique atmosphere.

True, there are larger hotels in this city, though I doubt , there are many more lovely. This smart boutique hotel offers stylish accommodation and the attention to detail is evident. Each room is completely individual, so there is bound to be one that suits.

There is an in house restaurant - the Olive Tree - careful, you may never want to leave the hotel !

Tel: 44 (0)1225 447928
web www.thequeensberry.co.uk

Rates - from £99.00 see website

Dorian House - 1 Upper Oldfield Park, Bath -BA2 3JX

This is one you really shouldn't miss. Set within a beautiful, period villa, a mere ten minute walk from the centre of Bath, Dorian House is really worth checking out.

The attention to detail is evident at every turn, from the marble bathrooms and pressure showers, to the Breakfast Orangery and the manicured gardens. This is the ideal base for touring this beautiful county, or simply chilling out in style.

Check out the website.

Tel +44(0)1225 426336
e mail info@dorianhouse.co.uk
web: www.dorianhouse.co.uk

Rates - £80 - £160

Features-
crisp cotton sheets
fluffy towels
tea/coffee making facilities
television
hairdryer & telephone

Bedfordshire

Luton Hoo - Hotel, Golf & Spa - The Mansion House, Luton, Bedfordshire - LU1 3TQ
This fine 5 star hotel and spa complex on the border of Hertfordshire and Bedfordshire really needs little introduction. Beyond the magnificent facade of the Mansion House which greets guests on arrival, lies a 5 star hotel, like no other in the home counties.

As one of the original luxury weekend retreats **Luton Hoo** certainly sets the standard for all the other luxury hotels There's a wide range of room and suite options to suit your taste and budget, and each one has been individually furnished and decorated to reflect its unique character, sometimes featuring silk lined and panelled walls, marble fireplaces and ornately decorated ceilings. Nearly all of the rooms also afford stunning views of the gardens and rolling parkland beyond.

The Parkland wing, a short walk from the Mansion House, has 38 air-conditioned bedrooms and suites, each equipped with flat-screen LCD television and broadband. Ground floor room and suites have their own private terraces, but to get the full effect of the sweeping views across the grounds the Roof Garden Suite is unmatched.
This is not a boutique hotel, but the last word in opulent accommodation.
Tel 44 (0)1582 734437
web: www.lutonhoo.co.uk

Rates – check out website
NB – this place is a great favourite for weddings and grand occasions, so can get really quite busy - be sure to double check your dates before booking.

Berkshire

The Forbury Hotel -26 The Forbury, Reading, Berkshire - RG1 3EJ

Evening Standard quote – 'The Forbury is 'The UK's Sexiest Townhouse Hotel' and the design and opulence is the talk of the fashionable set. From the 86,000 Italian glass beads in the chandelier running the height of the building in the old lift shaft, to the opulent fabrics and wallpapers and attention to every single detail - there is simply no place in the UK as extraordinarily opulent and stunning.

I think we can take it that they liked this hotel, and in Fairness, there is a lot to like - the bedrooms are chic, and the apartments superb - great base for taking in the many attractions of this area.

Tel: 01189 527 770
Web: www.theforburyhotel.co.uk

Rates - they have a huge range of offers via their website – check them out.

Cambridgeshire

Hotel Felix - Whitehouse Lane, Huntingdon Road, Cambridge - CB3 0LX.

More a classic comfort, than a boutique hotel. The 52 bedrooms have an elegant simplicity about them, with their King-Size Hypnos beds, Egyptian-cotton bed linen and duck down duvets.
The en-suite bathrooms are high quality, with many boasting walk-in Grohe rain shower and a bath.

All rooms have a mini bar with fresh milk for the tea and coffee making facilities, laptop safe, Satellite TV with Pay as you view movies, wi fi access, a data port for non networked laptop connections.

Tel: 44(0)1223 277977
web: www.hotelfelix.co.uk

Rates – Check out the website for some really unusual offers.

The Varsity – Thompson's Lane(off Bridge St), Cambridge – CB5 8AQ

The Varsity Hotel & Spa is located on the edge of the picturesque River Cam in the heart of Cambridge, so is ideally situated for punting, shopping, sight-seeing and nightlife in Cambridge.

Best described as classic chic, The Varsity has 48 individually themed rooms, many with terrific views over the city.

Tel: 44 (0)1223 30 60 30
Fax: +44 (0)1223 30 50 70

Reservations: info@thevarsityhotel.co.uk
web: www.thevarsityhotel.co.uk

Rates - POA

Features –

24 hour room service
concierge
DVD Library
full use of the gym facilities
in-room beauty treatment
complimentary Elemis Spa products
hairdressing

River Punting & Guided tours
Most rooms are air-conditioned (check on booking)

Cheshire

Kingsley Lodge - 10 Hough Lane. Wilmslow, Cheshire - SK9 2LQ

This is one boutique hotel you could so easily miss. Set in impressive gardens, Kingsley Lodge is a 3 minute drive to nearby Wilmslow, or 5 minutes to the pretty village of Alderley Edge.

This hotel has a small number of exquisitely designed guest bedrooms and suites, offering guests an experience of genuine exclusivity and the highest standards of personalised service.

Tel 44(0)1625 441794
web: www.kingsleylodge.com

Rates - Difficult to discover, contact for full details.

Oddfellows – 20 Lower Bridge Street, Chester - CH1 1RS

Situated in the very heart of historic Chester, Oddfellows offers 18 exclusive boutique bedrooms. Each individually themed, mixing iconic and contemporary furnishing styles.

From galleried bathrooms to circular beds, this certainly a hotel with a difference. There are several bar and dining areas within the hotel, so really could just stay indoors .

However, should you wish to explore Chester in more depth, you are ideally placed to do just that. Handy for all shopping, dining and entertainment, this one certainly ticks a lot of boxes.

We highly recommend you study the website to obtain the right room for your particular needs or taste.

Tel: 01244 895700
web: www.oddfellowschester.com

Rates – there are several offers and rates – ask

Features – dependent upon the room you book, here are some of the features inc'
rainwater shower
Nespresso machine
roll-top baths
audio visual equipment
large de-luxe beds

Hotel Dragonfly - 94 New Crane Street, (Watergate Street), Chester - CH1 2LF

The Dragonfly offers a minimilist/contemporary hotel set within a Grade II listed building. The location is perfect, just a few steps away from the famous Chester Racecourse, and less than five minutes to the centre of historic Chester, with its fine shops and restaurants.

Each room features an ultra-modern natural quarry slate en-suite bathroom with large showers, The deluxe rooms also have oversized bath tubs and large, fluffy white towels

This would make the perfect base for discovering Cheshire or North Wales - check out the website.

Tel: 01244 346 740
sleep@hoteldragonfly.com
web: www.hoteldragonfly.com

Rates - from £115.00

Cornwall

St Ives Harbour Hotel & Spa – Porthminster,
The Terrace, St.Ives, Cornwall - TR26 2BN

Set in a beautiful location by the sea, the 46 bedroom St Ives Harbour Hotel in St Ives, Cornwall enjoys stunning views across the Porthminster Bay.

Some rooms have balconies – a perfect place to relax over a lazy coffee and read. Great service, fine food and total relaxation - the essential ingredients for a perfect holiday in St Ives.
There are a variety of rooms to choose from, all of then finished to a very high standard.

Telephone 01736 795221
web: www.stives-harbour-hotel.co.uk

Rates – prices start from £145.00 (low season).

Old Quay House - Fowey, Cornwall - PL23 1AQ,

Anyone who has visited this prettiest of Cornish towns lately, can't have failed to notice, just how smart certain sectors of the hotel industry have become. Taking their lead from what the more discerning traveller has come to expect, they have risen to the challenge.

For those looking for a seaside retreat with that extra something, the architect designed and comfortably chic, Old Quay House, now fits the bill perfectly. Lovingly restored, and overlooking the town's attractive waterfront - it is one of the few boutique hotels in Cornwall to draw praise from all the major guide books year on year.

As a final bonus, the hotel also offers a varied menu in their restaurant area – one more good reason to head for Fowey.

Tel 01726 833302
web: www.theoldquayhouse.com

Rates – Classic double from £180.00

The Summer House Hotel - Cornwall Terrace, Penzance, Cornwall - TR18 4HL

They really don't come prettier than this. The attention to detail shown at this boutique hotel is truly outstanding. Main rooms are a happy marriage of seaside colours – squashy sofas and walls adorned with local art – this gracious old house gives itself over effortlessly to seaside living.

The walled garden is no less enchanting with its bright furniture, terracotta pots and palm trees. All bedrooms are en-suite with bath or shower and have TV, radio, DVD, wi-fi, hairdryer, tea & coffee trays, alarm clock, books, magazines etc.
Do check out the website – this is areal find!

Tel: 01736 363744
web: www.summerhouse-cornwall.com

Rates – Classic double from £120.00
NB - Open from April –October only.

Hotel Tresanton - St.Mawes, Cornwall -TR2-5DR

"If there is any more elegant hotel in Britain than Olga Polizzi's Tresanton on the Cornish Coast, then I have never been there" The-Independent
I'm afraid I have to agree, the village of St Mawes has always been a special place, and its beauty is only matched by the attention to detail shown at this prettiest of hotels. With its 31 rooms and suites, great bar areas and sea view terraces, you can forget about reality for a few days.

Stop press - they have now completed a fabulous Master Suite in Rock Cottage with wood burning stove, under-floor heating and a crow's nest terrace overlooking St Mawes Bay. There are also two houses, the Nook and Rock Cottage which are divided into individual rooms but can also be rented as a whole to accommodate an extended family or a party of friends. Special rates apply if the houses are taken as a whole.

Tel: 01326 270 055
web: www.tresanton.com/

Rates – Seaview doubles from £245.00 high season

The Scarlet Hotel - Tredragon Road, Mawgan Porth, Cornwall - TR8 4DQ

This is a strictly adults only hotel, so if you are thinking in family terms, this is not the place for you.

In their own words – '*Simply put, we are an award winning 37-bedroom hotel for adults, built to the highest eco standards, boasting delicious locally sourced food and the best Ayurvedic-inspired spa you can imagine*'.

We can't argue, located on a cliff-top location between Padstow and Newquay, this is certainly an impressive place. Each room is blessed with an outside space. The furnishings are sensational, the public spaces, something else, and the sea views – well, what can we say? The no children rule makes sense, when you see some of the balcony spaces (safety). This really is a divine place – we loved it.

Tel: 01637 861800
Fax: 01637 861801
web: www.scarlethotel.co.uk
email: stay@scarlethotel.co.uk

Rates – from £190

Upton House - 2 Esplanade, Fowey, Cornwall – PL23 1HY

Situated in the delightful town of Fowey, Cornwall, famous for its Regatta, and boating activities in general, Upton House certainly breaks the mould of traditional seaside accommodation.

If you like you hotel pink, silver and retro, then this is the place for you. Best described in the Hotel's own words –

'A unique air of 1940's Hollywood glamour greets you, the discerning traveller, and will make your stay the most romantic, sumptuous and decadent in Cornwall.

Indulge in pure 5 star luxury bed and breakfast accommodation with fine bespoke furnishings, handmade pocket sprung beds, roll top baths, rain showers and Penhaligon's Toiletries, just to mention a few. And your new love affair with Upton House need not end when you leave.

In our ground floor Boutique you can lose yourself and take Home the wonderful treasures that you have fallen in love with during your stay with us. If you're looking for a luxury boutique bed and breakfast in Fowey, Cornwall, then Upton House is the perfect place to stay.

Upton House is just for grown-ups, so leave the kids with grandma and come and enjoy yourselves without them for a few nights.'

We strongly recommend you check out the website

Tel: 01726 832732
web: www.upton-house.com

Rates – POA

Polurrian Bay Hotel - Polurrian Bay, Mullion, Cornwall, TR12 7EN

Looking for a family friendly Boutique Hotel? Then look no furher, for perched on a clifftop above Mounts Bay, sits the delightful Polurrian Bay Hotel. Totally re-furbished in 2011, The Polurrian combines child friendly facilities with a cool adult theme. Proving you can almost have it all.

You will find an array of child-friendly facilities including a free crèche for younger children and the Blue Room for the over eights. And for the parents there's a snug, a cinema, spa and on-site restaurants Set in 12 acres of glorious garden and with sublime views, you may never want to leave.
Check out the website

Tel: 01326 240421
web:www.polurrianhotel.com
e -mail: info@polurrianhotel.com

Rates - from £99.00 (low season)
Driftwood Hotel - Rosevine, Portscatho,Cornwall - TR2 5EW

Set in seven acres of private gardens, gradually layering down to the beach, a sheltered terrace with comfortable chairs, and a secluded weather boarded cabin overlooking the sea - this is the essence of Driftwood .

The rooms are stylishly decorated with TVs and videos. Ground floor bedrooms have their own decked terrace. The seaviews are complimentary.

Rates - POA

Check out the website

Tel: 44( )01872 580644
Fax: 01872 580801

e mailnfo@driftwoodhotel.co.uk
web:www.driftwoodhotel.co.uk

Headland House - Headland Road, Carbis Bay, St Ives , Cornwall - TR26

This luxury B&B is set within a pretty Edwardian three-story house, and sits on the headland above the glorious Carbis Bay, St Ives.

Lovingly restored and effortlessly designed, it combines all the modern conveniences you would expect, whilst retaining many of the obvious period features. There are six rooms, each one featuring king or superkingsize beds. The comfort continues with, goose down duvets and luxury bed linen.

This award winning B&B really is the place to step back from the everyday rigours of life.

Tel: 44(0)1736 796647
web: www.headlandhousehotel.co.uk

Rates - see website

Features -
tea and coffee making facilities
mini bar
flat screen TVs / integral dvd

Wi Fi

The Aramay - Aramay House, Quay Road, St Agnes, Cornwall - TR5 0RP

Stop Press
From 2013 the Aramay will be operating as Atlantic House offering luxury self-catering
with all the great bells an whistles you've come to expect.

For further information or details on how to book email :

hello@atlantichousecornwall.com

Tel: 44(0)1872 553546
web: www.thearamay.com

Rates – POA

The Boskerris - Boskerris Road, Carbis Bay, St Ives, Cornwall - TR26 2NQ

Boskerris is a delightful contemporary, boutique hotel with a relaxed Mediterranean style. Nestling on the edge of St Ives, it is discreetly set in one and a half acres, offering a unique position, with impressive views across St Ives Bay.

Sitting above the stunning Carbis Bay beach, this is the perfect spot to relax and unwind. Built in 1931 as a hotel, the Boskerris has always been privately run and has been totally transformed to blend contemporary cool with coastal comfort.

They offer three room types with most rooms facing the ocean. All their rooms are different sizes and have been individually designed.

Tel: 44(0)1736 795295
web: www.boskerrishotel.co.uk
Rates - from £125.00 (low season),

Check out the website

Features :
LCD TVs & DVD players + movies at reception
complimentary wi-fi access
White Company toiletries
soft fluffy towels, waffle bath robes & slippers

selection of teas & coffees, bottled mineral water
Pure digital radios
trademark Grohe showers either over the bath or
rainshower - glass or ceramic bowl basins
magazines, telephone & hairdryer
iron and ironing board on request

The Tide House - Skidden Hill, St Ives, Cornwall - TR26 2DU

The oldest hotel in St Ives in Cornwall, the Tide House has been lovingly restored, and is now luxury coastal bolt-hole. Dating from 1540, the granite fronted hotel nestles in a peaceful side street, yet is perfectly located for all restaurants, galleries and St Ive's award-winning beaches.

The Tide House has six very individual bedrooms, some with fabulous harbour views, and there are also stylish comfortable spaces for guests to relax. The Tide House is both family-friendly and a romantic retreat, a perfect place from which to discover St Ives and explore the wonderful Cornish coast.

Tel: 01736 791 803
web: www.thetidehouse.co.,uk

Rates - from £115 (low season - see website.

Talland Bay Hotel - Porthallow, Cornwall - PL13 2JB

Situated just 3 miles from Looe or Polperro, the Talland Bay Hotel is accessed via a delightful country lane that edges down to a sublime beach (two minute walk from the hotel).

The hotel has 22 rooms and the overall feel is one of designer comfort, and great detail. There is an 2AA Rosette restaurant and a delightful brasserie in house.

With sumptuous gardens and terraces, this is the ideal spot dicovering this beautiful county, or simply chilling out in comfort.

Tel: 44(0)1503 272667
web: www.tallandbayhotel.co.uk

Rates - from £120-.00 (low season)

Features
tea and coffee making facilities in all rooms

dressing Gowns in all rooms

hair dryers in all rooms
conference Facilities
private dining room
2AA Rossette restaurant open 6pm to 9.30pm
brasserie and bar menu

Treann House - 24 Dennis Road, Padstow, Cornwall - PL28 8DE

This stylish Edwardian town-house is a two minute stroll from Padstow Harbour. Completely refurbished in 2009, the Treann offers an immaculate mix of antiques and modern comfort. Though compact, just 3 en-suite rooms, this hotel / B&B offers the visitor a luxurious haven - the perfect base for discovering this ever popular county.

Highly recommended !

Tel: 44 (0) 1841 533 855
web: www.treannhousepadstow.co.uk

Rates - from £100.00 see website

Features
flat screen TV
DVD & CD player
digital radio & iPod dock

Cumbria

Gilpin Hotel & Lake House - Crook Road, Windermere – LA23 3NE

This privately owned and run hotel offers superb accommodation in a wonderful rural setting.

The update has been carried out without compromise, and offers a great standard of comfort – check out the website -

Tel: 015394 88818
web: www.gilpinlodge.co.uk

Rates – prices start from £260.00

Linthwaite House Hotel - Crook Road, Windermere - LA23 3JA, The Lake District

Linthwaite House Hotel is one of the AA's top 200 hotels, offering luxury accommodation and short breaks in the beautiful Lake District.

Situated in Windermere, it's ideal for walking, cycling or simply touring the Lake District. Close to all the major heritage attractions including: Beatrix Potter's 'Hilltop' and Wordsworth's homes, this is ideal retreat.

The bedrooms are a credit, and the views simply stunning.

Tel: 015394 88600
web: www.linthwaite.com

Rates – from £129.00 per person.

Windermere Suites, - New Road Windermere Cumbria - LA23 2LA

Whether you are planning a romantic weekend away, celebrating a special occasion or anniversary, searching for the perfect honeymoon or just looking for luxury accommodation in the heart of the Lake District, then this could be the answer.

They have just launched a range of experience stays to help you see the Lake District differently - through a lens, to high adrenaline adventure, or the county's artisan food producers, these experiences make a fantastic gift and can be combined with stays of 2 nights or more.

Tel: 015394 47672
web: www.windermeresuites.co.uk

Rates – from £185.00 per suite

Devon

Gidleigh Park - Chagford, Devon -TQ13 8HH

This award winning hotel offers Pure Indulgence at Gidleigh Park offers a break that provides the ultimate in luxurious extras, champagne in your room, a fabulous eight course signature menu and a wonderful ambience in which to relax and unwind, all set in glorious Devon countryside.

If you are a keen angler, or simply wish to learn, we can provide fishing licenses and tuition for the keen novice. Tackle and gear can be booked by prior arrangement.

Tel: 44(0)1647 432367
web: www.gidleigh.com

Rates – Classic rooms from £325.00

Browns Hotel - Dartmouth - 27-29 Victoria Road, Dartmouth, Devon – TQ6 9RT

Set in Dartmouth, Devon, Browns is a small boutique, privately run town-house hotel. During January and February of 2013 all the rooms have been refurnished and a number have been totally refurbished.

Browns has 8 individual rooms ranging from comfortable doubles to a large suite (possibly the largest hotel room in Dartmouth!). All the rooms are furnished in a modern style with great bath and shower rooms. This combined with top quality furnishings and original artworks, go to make this a very comfortable boutique hotel in a great location. One added advantage of this hotel is its excellent wine bar, dine and drink without leaving your hotel.

Tel 44 (0)1803 832572
web- www.brownshoteldartmouth.co.uk

Rates - from £145.00

Burgh Island Hotel - Bigbury-on-Sea, South Devon TQ7 4BG

If ever there was a place designed to heighten the sense of nostalgia and wellbeing, this is it. Built in 1929 for a prominent industrialist, and, since 2006, completely restored to its '30s glamour, the Burgh Island Hotel is a retreat like none other.

The beauty and intrigue of an island visit has always drawn guests who are looking for something different. It is no surprise therefore that such luminaries as Noel Coward, Agatha Christie and Lord Mountbatten stayed here.

I spent a weekend here some two years ago, and even in late autumn, the place is magical. The rooms, if you love art deco are great, and the public areas sublime. The food was excellent and the sea tractor to the island at high tide - great fun – try it !

Tel: 44 (0)1548 810514
web: www.burghisland.com

Rates – from £310.00

Plantation House - Totnes Road, Ermington, Devon – PL21 9NS

This privately owned, eight bedroom boutique hotel and restaurant, has a stylish yet relaxed atmosphere. Ideally located in the South Hams region of South Devon, it makes the perfect base for exploring this beautiful, rugged county.

The guestrooms are a delightful mix of contemporary and classic styles, creating a luxurious blend of discreet service and comfort.

In addition to the sumptuous guestrooms, the Plantation House boasts a delightful restaurant - (AA five star 'Restaurant with Rooms award).

Check out the website, this really is a find.

Tel:44 (0)1548 831100

e-mail info@plantationhousehotel.co.uk
web: www.plantationhousehotel.co.uk

Rates - POA

Southernhay House - 36 Southernhay East, Exeter EX1 1NX

'A chic, modern hotel and restaurant, inhabited by the ghosts of a Georgian past'
With just 10 bedrooms, a night at Southernhay is a personal experience, like having your own club in town. The Bar, Restaurant and Private Dining Room are simply the former grand salons of the original house and so are elegant and intimate in style, with limited covers and friendly, unhurried service.

All the bedrooms are individually styled, and the standard is exceptional. The dining experience attentive, and the location ideal for mooching or touring.

Tel: 01392 435 324
web: www.southernhayhouse.co.uk

Rates - from £150.00

Salcombe Harbour Hotel - Cliff Road, Salcombe, South-Devon - TQ8 8JH

Scheduled to re-opened in summer 2013, the 'Salcombe' has undergone a multi-million pound refurbishment. The first glimpse of the new-look hotel would seem to be impressive.

They recently released this statement -

'Harbour Hotels is delighted to announce that work on its Salcombe Harbour Hotel is now underway. Due to re-open its doors in Summer 2013, the multi-million pound project will include the installation of a luxury new Harbour Spa, with an indoor swimming pool and gymnasium, along with stunning new wedding and function room facilities, all with incredible Estuary views'.

We will watch this one for future reports, but it certainly looks good.
web: www.salcombe-harbour-hotel.co.uk
e-mail: salcombe@harbourhotels.co.uk

Tel: 01548 844444
Fax: 01548 843109

Dorset

Captain's Club Hotel - Wick Ferry, Wick Lane, Christchurch, Dorset - BH23 1HU

A contemporary maritime theme runs through this unusual hotel.
Its 29 rooms are split between 17 state bedrooms and 12 two or three bedroom suites. Each room has a stunning riverside view, air conditioning, flat screen TV with DVD players available upon request.

Its close proximity to the New Forest make it an ideal base for touring the area
Free high speed wireless broadband internet access is available in all rooms and throughout the hotel.

Tel: 44 (0)1202 475111
web: www.captainsclubhotel.com

Rates– State room from £229.00

Hotel Grosvenor - High Street, Shaftesbury, Dorset - SP7 8JA

Set in the beautiful Dorset town of Shaftesbury, this 16 roomed, upgraded hotel makes the perfect location for touring this beautiful county.
Each bedroom is individually decorated in a contemporary style with gorgeous curtains, giant headboards and crisp white 100% Italian cotton linen. Colours in the rooms range from warm greys, greens and stone shades, to deep aubergine with accents of hot reds and pinks.

The Greenhouse restaurant is headed by award winning Michelin star chef Mark Treasure. A Dorset man, Mark has previously worked in London hotels and restaurants such as The Capital Hotel, Mirabelle Restaurant, Cafe Royal and Langan's-Brasserie

Telephone: 01747 850580
web: www.hotelgrosvenor.com

Rates - standard rooms from £135.00

NB – check out the suites, well worth a glance

East Anglia

The Salt House Harbour Hotel - Neptune Quay, Ipswich, Suffolk - IP4 1AX

The Salthouse Harbour Hotel would best be described as a sexy hotel. It plainly goes beyond what you expect, and exudes its 4 star status in every curious corner, from eccentric sofas and unstuffy cushion., to the sea-salted brickwork exterior

Now a ship-shape contemporary warehouse of rich modern interiors and rooms adorned with vintage furniture, sculptures and eclectic art. The staff are professionally attentive to your every need, and the cuisine exciting. Great location - should fill a hectic weekend.

Tel; 01473 226789
web: www.salthouseharbour.co.uk
Rates – see website

Essex

Pier View - Royal Terrace, Southend-on-Sea, Essex. SS1 1DY

Overlooking the Pier and sea front in the conservation area of Southend-on-Sea and just off Pier Hill, this pretty hotel has undergone refurbishment to a fine standard.

All rooms feature wall mounted LCD television, free Wi-Fi access and tea and coffee making facilities.

Its close proximity to shops and restaurants make it an ideal stay for discovering Essex. Easy access to the A127 and M25 (Plenty of parking close to the property)

Tel: 44(0)1702 437900
web: www.pierviewguesthouse.co.uk

Rates - From £99.00 inc breakfast
.

Gloucestershire

Cotswold House Hotel & Spa - The Square,
Chipping Campden, Gloucestershire - GL55 6AN

This luxury Hotel and Spa in the heart of Chipping Campden, Gloucestershire, is one of the most beautiful hotels in the area, and makes a perfect base for discovering this lovely county.

Choose from Standard and Deluxe King Rooms, Cottage Rooms, Junior Suites or two luxurious Suites, all overlooking the hotel garden. This hotel has exceptionally good reviews.

Tel: 44(0)1386 840330
web: www.cotswoldhouse.com

Rates – There are spa packages and a variety of different rate – check website

Barnsley House - Barnsley, Cirencester, Gloucestershire - GL7 5EE

This Cotswold stone manor house set in stunning gardens, is perfect for that complete getaway weekend, or a luxurious base for touring this beautiful county.

Each room has a bespoke touch that lives in perfect harmony with this unique building. From fluffy towel robes and twin tubs to entertainment systems and romantic lighting, they've taken care of every detail. We liked this one.

Tel: 01285 740 000
web: www.barnsleyhouse.co.uk

Rates – from £350.00

Cowley Manor – Cowley, Nr Cheltenham, Gloucestershire – GL53 9NL

If you like your country house or manor to have a modern twist, then this one is probably for you. The exterior of the grand house and estate gives every impression of a classical building set in glorious parklands. Once inside, that illusion rapidly disappears, to be replaced by state-of-the art furnishings and contemporary colours - even the billiard table baize is blue.

The modern theme extends throughout the public areas and the bedrooms. This really is a very brave move, and you will either love it or hate it – we advise you to check out the website prior to making your reservation.

Tel: 01242 870 900
web: www.cowleymanor.com

Rates – start from £175.00

Thirty Two Hotel - 32 Imperial Square, Cheltenham, Gloucestershire - GL50 1QZ

This prettiest of boutique hotels is set in a Regency terrace overlooking Imperial Gardens. Thirty Two provides a quiet and exclusive haven that would impress even the most discerning traveller. The 5 star accommodation comes with private parking and is within 2 minutes walk of Cheltenham's best shops, hotels, restaurants & bars

No expense has been spared in fitting out this unique hotel – from the exquisite suites to the public rooms, the attention to detail is simply first class.

Tel: 44 (0)1242 771110
web: www.thirtytwoltd.com

Features –
Egyptian cotton linens
pocket sprung beds

goose down duvets and pillows
beautiful natural stone bathrooms
rain showers
Penhaligon[1]s toiletries
fluffy white robes

Rates – from £160.00

Cotswold 88 Hotel - Kemps Lane, Painswick - GL6 6YB

Here, once again, the historic exterior hides a truly funky hotel. A fusion of colour and stripes await the visitor.
In line with the current trend, that every country house deserves a make-over, this one doesn't disappoint.

We have had good reports from those who have stayed here - our one big criticism is the website – too clever, and really doesn't show this unique hotel to its best. You have to dig deep to get actual images. We still like it though !

Tel; 01452 813688
Web: www.cotswolds88hotel.com

Rates – start at a very reasonable £110.00 B&B

The Montpellier Chapter - Bayshill Road, Montpellier
Cheltenham – GL50 3AS

Set in a stunning white classic mansion house in the
Montpellier district of Cheltenham, this hotel sets the
benchmark for pure elegance with a modern twist. They
have simply got it right from every aspect.

Step inside the hotel and you move from the restored
character of the Villa with its warm, intimate bar, open
fireplaces and library to the light and airy garden room.
The conservatory, a local landmark, carefully restored,
is a great place to take tea.

Move onto the bedrooms and from standard rooms to
the glorious penthouse, you realize what good taste is,
and this place just oozes it.

Tel: 01242 527788
web:
www.themontpellierchapterhotel.com

Rates - there are various deals and special feature
events to be had – check out the website for details.

Gt Manchester

Didsbury House Hotel - Didsbury Park, Didsbury Village, Manchester - M20 5LJ

Set in a beautiful white, large Victorian House, Didsbury House offers twenty three bedrooms and four suites varying in size and style.

Each room offers comfort and style ranging from the bijou snug Classic to the more popular and larger Eclectic Villas and Duplex rooms, whilst our more indulgent guests may choose to stay in our Duplex Junior Suites or Loft Suites.

In addition they offer a wide variety of packages and event management, including - weddings, conferences, private parties etc.

Tel: 0161 448 2200
Web: www.eclectichotels.co.uk/didsbury-house

Rates - start from £71.00 – though they do have a baffling array of prices – check out website.

Great John Street Hotel – Great John St, Manchester

Part of the Eclectic Group, this hotel is perfectly positioned for shops, restaurants and theatres. This original Victorian school house has been transformed into a chic townhouse hotel, with unique, individually designed bedrooms and suites, alongside stylish lounges and Oyster Bar.

Great John Street also boasts stunning entertainment rooms and features Manchester's only Eclectic Roof Terrace (available for exclusive use for your own tailor made event.)

Tel: 0161 831 3211
web:
www.eclectichotels.co.uk/great-johnstreet

Rate- once again, rates are very varied – check out website

Macdonalds Townhouse Manchester - 101 Portland Street Manchester - M1 6DF

This stylish hotel is set in a grade II listed building at the very heart of Manchester. This is the perfect location for all restaurants, bars, clubs, shopping and theatre.

The Macdonald Townhouse boasts a huge 85 rooms, not our usual quota, but this is city centre hotel.
As you would expect, all the rooms are equipped with the latest facilities.

Tel 0844 855 9136
web: www.macdonaldhotels.co.uk

Rates - check out the website for deals.

Malmaison Manchester - Gore Street | Piccadilly, Manchester M1 3AQ

Malmaison Manchester has 167 super-slinky rooms and all rooms have the complete set of Mal ingredients - great beds, mood lighting, en-suite bathrooms with baths and power showers, CD players, satellite TV, and serious wines. Other little touches include same-day laundry service, exclusive toiletries (that you're encouraged to take with you), 24 hour room service, fast and free internet access.

Malmaison is ideally situated for Piccadilly station and central Manchester's bars, restaurants and theatres.

Tel: 0161 278 1000
Web: www.malmaison.com

Rates – check out the website for events and offers
.

Hampshire

Lyme Wood Hotel - Beaulieu Road, Lyndhurst-SO43-7FZ

If you want the best and money is not a consideration, then look no further. When I visited, my budget only stretched to coffee and cakes on the rear terrace. That was enough to convince me, that here is somewhere rather special.

The setting is stunning. Following a huge restoration and re-furb, this has become probably the premier hotel of the area

Tel: 44 (0)2380 287- 1 77
web: www.limewoodhotel.co.uk

Rates – POA

Aviator -Farnborough Road, Farnborough, Hampshire, GU14 6EL

Aviator was created by TAG Group as a hotel for elite travellers moving between London and the world's leading destinations. Located in Farnborough, Hampshire, Aviator opened in 2008 as one of the most striking design hotels in recent times

Rooms & Suites - interiors are contemporary yet rich and comfortable, with walnut panelling, leather accented furniture and wet rooms with black glass walls, granite vanity tops and chrome finishing. Complimentary movies, music library and wifi are included for all guests.

Tel: 44 (0)1252 555 890
Web: www.aviatorbytag.com

Rates – On application

The Master Builder's Hotel - Buckler's Hard, Beaulieu
Estate, Hampshire - SO42 7XB

Set in the delightful village of Buckler Hard an 18th
century shipbuilding village on the banks of the
Beaulieu River, in the heart of the New Forest National
Park, Hampshire. The Master Builder's is a delightful
boutique hotel, offering quality accomodation and also
has a bar and restaurant.

The Luxury Rooms in the main house, are individually
created by the well-known interior designer Christine
Boswell. Their are also Classic Rooms available in the
Henry Adams wing.

The Masterbuilder's also has a seperate cottage
available and includes - The Cottage has one double
room upstairs, with a twin bedded room accessed via an
inter-connecting door. Downstairs, there is a bathroom
with a shower above the bath, a double sofa bed in the
sitting room, next to which is a dining room with a table
and eight chairs.
The kitchen includes a fridge, cooker with hob,
microwave and a dishwasher.

Tel: 44 (0)844 815 3399
web: www. themasterbuilders.co.uk

Rates - from £130.00

Herefordshire

Castle House - Castle Street, Hereford - HR1 2NW

Tucked away in the most elegant quarter of Hereford and within two minutes walk of the magnificent Hereford Cathedral.

Castle House is a unique, highly recommended, privately-owned boutique townhouse hotel. Certainly the most luxurious and prestigious hotel in the area.

With its Georgian architecture, 24 individually-themed suites and bedrooms, and a terraced garden leading down to the tranquil Castle Moat, Castle House has a very special relaxed and informal atmosphere.

Tel: 44 (0) 1432 356321
web: www.castlehse.co.uk

Rates – Single rooms from £130.00

Isle of Wight

The Hambrough - Hambrough Rd, Ventnor, Isle Of Wight PO38 1SQ

This unique boutique hotel is run by the acclaimed chef Robert Thompson.

The hotel offers a very different approach to the norm, stylish rooms with all the up to date spec' you could wish for, with the added bonus of a first class restaurant in-house.

Tel: 01983 856333
web: www.robert-thompson.com

Rates - POA

Hillside - 151 Mitchell Avenue, Ventnor,
Isle of Wight - PO38 1DR

A mere ten minute walk from the beach will bring you to this delightful hotel. Hillside was extensively refurb - ished in Spring/Summer 2009 and now offers a minimalistic Scandinavian interior in which to feel at home.

All rooms are en-suite, and finished to a superior-standard   .

Check out the website – this really is a find.
Rates start from as little as £69.00

Tel: 44(0)1983 852271
web: www.hillsideventnor.co.uk

Rates – once gain it would be best to check them out on their website

Kent

Rowhill Grange Hotel & Utopia Spa –Wilmington, Kent - DA2 7QH

This 18th century country house is Ideally situated and is a mere ½hr or so by train from London central. On offer is everything from spa weekends to fine dining.

With personally selected designer fabrics, elegant solid-wood furnishings and four-poster or sleigh beds fitted with sumptuous, deep sprung mattresses, plush pillows and the finest Egyptian cotton sheets, , I think you will sleep soundly .

Tel: 44 (0)1322 615136
web: www.alexanderhotels.co.uk/rowhil

Rates - deals from £109 per person - check out website
All rates are inclusive of WiFi and temporary membership of the Utopia Spa

The Brew House Hotel - 1 Warwick Park, Royal
Tunbridge Wells, Kent - TN2 5TA

The Brew House boutique hotel is located close to the
historic Pantiles area of Royal Tunbridge Wells , and has
been described one of the top boutique hotels in Kent.
This 15 bedroom, uba-smooth hotel would make a
perfect base for the beautiful county of Kent.

Tel: 01892 520587
web: www.thebrewhousehotel.net

Features –
luxurious queen size double bed
flat screen lcd or Bang & Olufsen tv
radio or ipod dock
fully air conditioned
international direct dial telephone
free wifi access
tea & coffee making facilities
hairdryer and ironing board
electronic safe
ensuite bathrooms (with shower and/or
bath) and complimentary toiletries –
look out for the "magical" smart glass
in some of our bedrooms

Rates - POA

The Bell Hotel – The Quay, Sandwich, Kent – CT13 9EF

For those visiting Kent, you could do worse than make Sandwich your base, and really you need look no further than the Bell Hotel. There's a choice of bedrooms consisting of single, twin, double rooms and suites. Some bedrooms have balconies and river views, while others overlook the rooftops of this delightful town.

All the rooms are individually designed, and would probably be best described as classic, with a designer-twist, and full en-suite facilities. The Bell has the added advantage of great in housed food, via their brasserie and dining menus + an impressive selection of quality wines.

Tel: 44 (0) 1304 61 33 88
web: www.thebellhotelsandwich.co.uk

Rates – from £110.00
Features:
bespoke toiletries
hair dryers
coffee and tea making facilities
digital radios
remote controlled televisions
telephones
free WI FI access throughout the hotel.

The Front Rooms - 9 Tower Parade, Whitstable, Kent
CT5 2BJ

If you are looking for a base from which to discover more about this beautiful county, or simply a cool place to chill out for a few days, then look no further.

The Front Rooms is situated in the historic seaside town of Whitstable on the Kent coast. This family-run boutique B&B has been lovingly created with your comfort and relaxation in mind, with light and airy guestrooms. There are three double rooms (2 en-suite, 1 private shower) featuring - Victorian cast-iron double beds, made up with crisp Egyptian cotton bed linen and cosy blanket throws.

Rates - from £110.00

Features:
luxury toiletries
soft white towels and bathrobes
library of books & dvds,

Lancashire

Inglewood Boutique - B & B 19 Southport Road, Chorley, Lancashire - PR7 1LB.

Probably not the first place you would first look for a boutique hotel or B&B. However, it's obvious that Inglewood, this large Edwardian Townhouse has been lovingly restored, and now provides a mixture of traditional features with up-to-date facilities .

Comfortable beds, elegant rooms, and gorgeous bedding, go to make for a great experience at a modest price. A short stroll takes you to the shops, pubs, and restaurants – a perfect base for discovering the great Lancashire countryside.

Tel: 07792 957168
web: www.inglewoodboutiquebandb.co.uk

Rates – from £62.00

The Ashton - Wyresdale Road, Lancaster - LA1 3JJ

Lancaster today is a world away from its semi industrial past, the areas around the river and the old quays, are positively humming with restaurants, bars and general life. Set on the edge of this fine city, and handy for the beautiful Trough of Bowland, The Ashton makes the perfect base for your Lancashire staycation

The Ashton has 5 bedrooms spread over several floors. each individually designed,   and all featuring the facilities you'd expect to find in a luxury hotel. Whether you choose a Grand Room and bathe in glamour or opt for a Cosy Classic, they appear to have thought of every detail, including the views over Williamson Park and the famous Ashton Memorial.

Breakfast at the Ashton is a joy, and afterwards, you can head for the sitting room with its squashy sofas, papers and books, or you may prefer to relax in the lawned garden.
Tel 01524 68460

web: www.theashtonlancaster.com

Rates – classic room from £125.00

NB – there are plays in Williamson Park during the month of July – so check in advance.

The Midland Morecambe - Marine Road West, Morecambe, Lancashire - LA4 4BU

This sleepy seaside town may not be the first place you would think of for a boutique hotel stay. Well, if you are thinking of touring the lakes or deepest Lancashire, this newly renovated, Art Deco hotel, could be just the ticket.

In its heyday the Midland was the first port of call for any star or dignitary visiting this popular destination. The hotel has been lovingly restored. Smart and gleaming, the outer facade looks very similar to the original, but inside, there is barely a room that hasn't been re-vamped. We're pleased to see, that despite such extensive work, they have managed to retain many of the original features, such as the wide, spiral staircase, and the wonderful circular ceiling-panel by the renowned sculptor Eric Gill.

All in all, the place is a triumph, and makes the perfect luxury base for your Lake / Lancashire weekend.

Tel: 08458 501 240
web:www.englishlakes.co.uk

Rates – POA

Northcote - Northcote Road, Langho, Blackburn,,
Lancashire - BB6 8BE

Not so much a country house hotel, more a wonderful
restaurant with fabulous rooms. The moment you enter
Northcote, you get the distinct feeling that the driving
forces behind this establishment knows exactly what
they are doing.

The bedrooms are sumptuous, as is the dining area.
There are countless options from gourmet weekends to
private parties and more. As if this were not enough you
are within driving distance of some of the most glorious
countryside anywhere in the UK.

Tel: 01254 240555
web: www.northcote.com

Rates – from £255.00

Number One, St Luke's - 1 St Luke's Road, Blackpool
Lanc's - FY4 2EL

Hosts Mark and Claire Smith have a wealth of experience as hoteliers and are dedicated to making every guest's visit a memorable one. Number One makes the ideal base for discovering the wonderful county of Lancashire or simply having fun in Blackpool.

This is a very stylish alternative to the usual seaside offering. From the deluxe beds and bedding, to the remote lighting, they have thought of everything - check out the website !

Tel: 44(0)1253 343901
e-mail: info@numberoneblackpool.com
web: www.numberoneblackpool.com

Rates- from £70.00 (single occupancy)

Features
42" plasma TV screens
Sony PlayStation2
Freeview, Wi-fi,
remote lighting
refreshment trays

ensuite bathroom including a Whirlpool bath & 17" LCD
TV, power shower
music system

.

Park House - Church View, Gisburn, Clitheroe, Lanc's BB7 4HG

Set within the glorious Ribble Valley, Park House is a luxury Boutique B&B and in their own words - 'Combining Georgian elegance with touches of contemporary style.'

There's certainly plenty of style about this residence. What it lacks in size, it more than makes up for in its complete attention to detail.

From the sumptuous beds to the elegant bathrooms and reception areas, this hotel carries the mark of people who care deeply about the hotel and their clients.

Check out the website

Tel: 44(0)1200 445269
web: www.parkhousegisburn.co.uk

Rates – POA

The Villas Residence - No 2 Oakenrod Villas, Bury Road, Rochdale - OL11 4EE

The words Boutique Hotel are often misused when describing sometimes very mundane hotels, so believe us when we say this is a 'Boutique Hotel' in every sense of the words. Each room is styled on a particular era.

In less capable hands, this idea could have been a complete disaster, but in the case of the 'The Villas Residence', it is a complete triumph. From the Tudor and Victorian rooms through to the exquisite Art-Deco suite, the attention to detail is simply delightful.

So if you are looking for a base from which to discover the wonderful Lancashire countryside, or maybe you wish to simply step back in time to a more relaxed lifestyle - then look no further.

Take a good look at the website !

Tel:44 (0)1706 525075
web: www.the-villas-residence.co.uk

Rates – POA

London

Sanctum Soho Hotel – 20 Warwick Street, Soho, London - W18 5NF

Developed from two Georgian town houses, this sumptuous hotel is ideally located for all the West End can offer, including Regent Street, Bond Street and Liberty's dep't store.

There are 30 guest rooms, roof terrace and bars, all styled to perfection. You really do leave the world outside when you enter this establishment.

They also offer access to a personal shopper, gym, limousines, and in-room spa treatments.

Tel: 44 (0)207 292 6101
web: www.sanctumsoho.com

Rates - via website

Shoreditch House - Ebor Street Shoreditch London - E1 6AW

This is probably one of the most unusual places to stay in London. Don't be put off by the exterior, or the immediate interior, for once you ascend to the main area of this hotel/members club – like stepping into Willy Wonka's Chocolate Factory, the whole place opens up into floor after floor of pure fantasy .

The bedrooms are bijou but oh so nice. And for your delight, there is a cinema, bowling alley, Cowshed spa, rooftop swimming pool, gymnasium, chill areas, cocktail bars and restaurants.

Don't be surprised if you bump into the odd celeb' - pre-booking essential - check out the website - simply great. We loved this one - happy staff -check out the cocktails

Tel: 44(0)20 7739 5040
web: www.shoreditchhouse.com

Rates - Non members from £245.00

Bulgari Hotel & Residences London – 171
Knightsbridge, London – SW7 1DW

The 85 rooms and suites at the Bulgari Hotel & Residences are simply stunning. They are spacious (in fact, among the largest available in London).

With views over Hyde Park and Knightsbridge, each one is an oasis of comfort and sleek luxury. Bulgari's renowned attention to detail is evident at every turn. With the use of exquisite marbles, fine woods and unique detailing, blended with English style and Italian heritage, the Bulgari is something very special.

The large bathrooms feature free-standing baths and showers in exquisite Marquina marble and white glass. Each bedroom offers a 42" LCD TV with connections for guest media devices, Nespresso coffee machine, complimentary wireless Internet and the usual Bulgari amenities.

The Bulgari Spa provides a rare comprehensive spa experience in the heart of London. Set over two entire floors the Spa comprises a 25m swimming pool, vitality pool, thermal experiences with ice fountains and cooling showers, relaxation room, 11 treatment rooms offering exclusive bespoke Bulgari treatments for the face and body, a fully equipped fitness centre and nail salon.

Set in the heart of Knightsbridge, London's newest and finest luxury hotel is sure to prove a winner.

Tel: 44(0)207 151 1010

web: www.bulgarihotels.com
Rates: Rooms POA
Suites from £1560.00 per night

Number Sixteen- 16 Sumner Place, London - SW7 3EG

Number Sixteen is situated in the heart of South Kensington. So is ideal for the Victoria & Albert and Natural History museums, and is within easy reach of Kensington Gardens, Knightsbridge and Harrods.

The rooms are nothing short of delicious, as are the public areas. There is a secluded garden, just perfect for afternoon tea.

This is the perfect escape from the busy world outside – Recommended *

Tel: 020 7589 5232
web: www.firmdalehotels.com/london/number-sixteen

Rates – double room from £185.00

Citizen M - 20 Lavington Street, London -SE1 0NZ

I know, the name sounds like something from a George Orwell novel, but If you like your hotels ultra-funky and really off the wall, then look no further.

This centrally located boutique hotel, is definitely not the place your grandmother would take to. The bedrooms are a mixture of high tech meets funky light show. While the public areas make the bedrooms look positively sedate.
You really must check out this hotel's website - ike Marmite - you will simply love it or hate it.

Tel: 44 203 519 1680
web: www.citizenm.com

Rates – from £113.00

NB - Reservations can only be made online, with a valid credit card

The Soho Hotel - 4 Richmond Mews, London - W1D 3DH

Part of Firmdale Hotels, The Soho Hotel is situated in a quiet mews between Dean and Wardour Streets in the heart of Soho, London. The Nearest tube stations are Oxford Circus, Tottenham Court Road or Piccadilly Circus. The perfect location for your stay in London

From standard rooms to suites and apartments, the Soho leaves nothing to chance. The décor is stunning, the attention to detail exceptional and the ambience – well, near perfect.

There are a number of reception rooms, a drawing room (with honesty bar) and library, 2 cinemas and a gym for guests' use. This really is a hotel for the 21st century.

Tel: 44 020 7559 3000
web: www.firmdalehotels.com/london/the-soho-hotel

Rates - from £295.00

NB – watch the price of the honesty bar drinks – ouch !

Eccleston Square Hotel - 37 Eccleston Square, London - UK SW1V 1

Set within a delightful Georgian square - Eccleston Square Hotel is located on the border of Belgravia and Victoria, within walking distance of Victoria, with its transport connections and theatres. All 39 rooms are equipped with electrically adjustable Hästens massage beds, the latest 46-inch Panasonic 3D LED TV, complimentary 3D blu-ray movie library, VoIP phones, high pressure rainfall showers and a programmable 'wake up and sleep' experience.

All rooms feature the iPad 2, from which guests can control. If you like your rooms chic and the latest of all mod-cons, swish bars and dining areas, this could be just the place for you

Rates from - £195.00

Tel: 020 3489 1000
web: www.ecclestonsquarehotel.com

The Fox Club - 48 Clarges Street, London - W1J 7ER

If you are a regular visitor to London, it may be worth checking this one out. The rooms are classically sumptuous, with deep sprung beds, Egyptian cotton sheets and luxurious toiletries.

A little history - 'The Fox Club takes its name from one of the former residents of 46 Clarges Street. In the 18th century, Charles James Fox was a renowned statesman, political giant and civil liberty campaigner. In his later years he lived at these premises with his courtesan lover and wife, Mrs Armistead'.

Conveniently placed, just off Piccadilly, you are in the very heart of London, with all the comforts of home.

Tel: 020 7495 3656
web: www.foxclublondon.com

Rates - exec' doubles from £174.00 (member's price.)

Café Royal – 68 Regent Street, London - W1B 4DY

The Café Royal has reopened as a luxury 5 star hotel. Situated in the heart of central London (you really can't get more central than this), this historic building holds a special place in the heart of Londoners.

With elegant Mayfair to the west and creative Soho to the east, Café Royal hotel is perfectly positioned within walking distance of London's finest shopping streets, such as Bond St, Regent St, and the delightful streets of Mayfair. Perfect for all restaurants and theatres, this has to be one of the most convenient places to stay whilst in London.

In addition to the collection of modern and high detail finished bedrooms and suites, Café Royal hotel also boasts six Historic Suites, each with their own aesthetic, character and story. All bedrooms and suites are superbly equipped and feature; Egyptian cotton bed linen, a fully stocked Butler's Pantry and Bang & Olufsen media systems.

In view of the short length of time this hotel has been open, there is little feedback to be had. Although, it goes without saying that if you study the website, and based on our own initial contact via the front desk etc – this looks a very promising venue – Must be worth a try.

Rates – from £310.00
Worth checking out some of the 'Dine & Stay' offers.

Telephone +44 (0)20 7406 3333
Fax +44 (0)20 7406 3366web:
www.hotelcaferoyal.com
Reservations +44 (0)20 7406 3322

High Road House - 162-170 Chiswick High Road London W4 1PR UK

Opened in 2006, High Road House, this oh so chic hotel and members' club can be found on Chiswick High Road W4. It boasts 14 small but well-equipped bedrooms, upstairs at the House is an intimate restaurant and bar, while downstairs is a space for members' events and private parties.

High Road House is just 20 minutes from both Heathrow Airport and central London.

This looks a very attractive proposition if you prefer to be just a little out of town - certainly well worth a look.

Rates - POA

Tel: 020 8742 1717
web: www.highroadhouse.co.uk

Sanderson - 50 Berners Street , London - W1 3NG

The Sanderson is best described in their own words -
'A lavish "Urban Spa" in the heart of London's West End,
Sanderson offers a retreat from the bustle of the city
into a world of fantasy and wellbeing.

This landmark 50s building has been transformed by
Philippe Starck into a surreal Cocteau-like dream world,
epitomizing a "new luxury" that is smart, pared down,
and tempered with a healthy dose of wit and irony. With
the absence of "normal" walls and a floor-to-ceiling
glass facade that diffuses natural light through flowing
layers of ethereal sheer curtains, Sanderson's
indoor/outdoor lobby is a layered and sophisticated
environment that is totally original.

Surrounding an extraordinary landmark Courtyard
Garden designed by Philip Hicks, Starck's visionary style
mixes baroque and modern, juxtaposing Salvador Dali's
curvaceous red lips sofa with classic 60s mosaics and
hand-carved African furniture with an oversized Louis
XV armoire. The result blends wit, magic and surprise in
an elegant balancing act of extravagance'

Sounds pretty impressive - certainly one for the lovers
of Uber -Smooth.

Tel: 020 7300 1400
web: www.sandersonlondon.com

Rates – POA

Adria Boutique Hotel - 88 Queens Gate, London - SW7 5AB.

The Adria is a remodeled Victorian townhouse, originally built in 1870. The hotel has 22 guestrooms and 2 suites. Rooms are not "numbered", but "lettered" with "A" being Adria each room follows alphabetically so you can stay in the Bowler (B), the Croquet (C), the Downing (D), the Elizabeth (E), the Fortnum (F) rooms with variations continuing until "Z".

Each room is different in design and feel and includes original commemorative momentos corresponding to the room title. This stylish boutique hotel offers everything the modern discerning guest has come to expect.

From marble bathrooms with underfloor heating and walk-in waterfall showers (in each luxury room) to your own espresso machine, iPod dock, and a HD iMedia hub. - the Adrai has it.

Their philosophy and mission, they state, ' is to create a home away from home" - we think they may have done just that, see what you think.

Tel:44 (0)207 1188988/9.
e mail:stay@theadria.com
web: www.theadria.com

Merseyside

Hotel Indigo Liverpool - 10 Chapel Street
Liverpool - L3 9AG

If you like your hotels bright and funky, stop now - this 151 bedroom hotel 4-star hotel situated in the city's commercial district is a mere 5 minute journey from the BT convention centre and the Echo Arena.

Guestrooms come complete with oversized beds, spa-inspired bathrooms and complimentary wireless internet access.
Be sure to check out the website – this one is not for all tastes.

Tel: 0151 559 0111
web: www.hotelindigoliverpool.co.uk
Rates – POA via website

Oxfordshire

Hope House - Oxford Street, Woodstock - OX20 1TS

Set in the delightful Oxfordshire village of Woodstock and within walking distance of the spectacular Blenheim Palace, it was obvious that this boutique hotel would carry a Marlborough theme.

That said, this place does manage the sometimes difficult task of blending old and new. There is just enough updating to make you feel in touch, without taking away from the building's obvious charms.
The perfect location for a great weekend or the ideal base for touring this fine county.

Tel: 44 (0)1993 815990
Web: www.hopehousewoodstock.co.uk

Rates – on application

Old Parsonage Hotel - 1 Banbury Road Oxford - OX2 6NN

The independently owned Old Parsonage Hotel, situated in St Giles, dates back to the 1660. Though, the minute you walk through the front entrance you are definitely brought into the 21st century.

The decor is sumptuous classic with a contemporary twist, instilling a very relaxed and comfortable feel. This is reinforced by the attentive service on offer.

The Old Parsonage is the perfect spot for that chill-out weekend in glorious Oxford.

Tel: 01865 310210
web: www.oldparsonage-hotel.co.uk

Rates – POA

Scotland

Remember, Edinburgh plays host to an annual Festival and a Military Tatoo, it's worth checking your dates when planning your break.

Hotel Missoni - 1 George IV Bridge, Edinburg - EH1 1AD

One of Edinburgh's latest hotels, its 136 rooms and suites offer ultra hip boutique styling, stylish cocktail bar and restaurant. It is conveniently situated on The Royal Mile, in Edinburgh's historic centre.

I enjoyed the stay, the bar and breakfast areas were enjoyable, and if you like hip hotels, then this may be the one for you.

Tel: 44 (0)131 2206666
web: www.hotelmissoni.com

Rates available via website.

21212 - 3 Royal Terrace, Edinburgh - EH7 5AB

This multi-award winning restaurant, now has the added advantage of four sumptuously appointed bedrooms The four large bedrooms, with dedicated lounge areas, are split over the two upper levels of the house, offering commanding views over the gardens to the rear, and stunning views of the city of Edinburgh to the front.

On a clear day, bedrooms 1 and 21 also offer views to the Firth of Forth and beyond.

Each bedroom's decor is individually designed, and facilities include en-suite bathrooms with either a free-standing bath and walk-in shower or a specially designed wet room. Guests also have their own flat-screen plasma television, internet connection and extensive storage spaces.

All four bedrooms, are available seven nights a week.

Tel: 44 (0)131 523 1030
web: www.21212restaurant.co.uk

Rates – see website.

The Bonham Hotel - 35 Drumsheugh Gardens.
Edinburgh. Scotland - EH3 7RN

The Drumsheugh Gardens triangle was built between 1874 and 1882. The three storey residences were quickly recognised as "des-res" in Edinburgh terms.

Now the home of 'The Bonham,' a luxury boutique hotel, where you'll find contemporary ambiance, mixed with classic style, that sits well within this impressive Victorian town-house. The bedrooms are colourful and stylish, and come with en-suite bathrooms and over-bath showers.

Central location and free car parking.

Tel: +44 (0) 131 226 6050
web: www.townhousecompany.com/thebonham

Rates – superior double from £155.00

94DR - 94 Dalkeith Road Edinburgh - EH16 5AF

Approx 10 min's south side of Edinburgh, 94 DR is a 7 bedroom boutique guest house that ticks all the right boxes

Individually designed rooms offer everything from power showers and white linen towels to LCD televisions, and DVD player. The attention to detail throughout is exceptional, and is topped off by the importance this hotel places on a 'Good Breakfast'.
Do check out the website
Tel: 0131 662 9265

web: www.94dr.com

Rates: from £80.00

NB – the owners are obviously well clued up when it comes to Edinburgh life- don't be afraid to ask for their help.

Citizen M - 60 Renfrew Street, (corner of Hope Street, Glasgow, Scotland - G2 3BW

I know, the name sounds like something from a George Orwell novel, but If you like your hotels ultra-funky and really off the wall, then look no further.

This centrally located boutique hotel, is definitely not the place your grandmother would take to. The bedrooms are a mixture of high tech meets funky light show. While the public areas make the bedrooms look positively sedate.
You really must check out this hotel's website – like Marmite – you will simply love it or hate it.

Tel: 44 203 519 1111
web: www.citizenm.com/glasgow

Rates – Various from £113.00

NB - Reservations can only be made online, with a valid credit card

15 Glasgow – 15 Woodside Place, Glasgow – G3 7QL

This truly is a boutique hotel in every sense of the word. Glasgow's latest luxury bed and breakfast hotel. Situated on the edge of Glasgow city centre and a breath away from the heart of the West End, 15 is a welcome newcomer.

There are just five rooms, although they are more like suites, as each one is completely individual, and finished to an exacting standard - someone here really loves their business.

The Lister room, finished completely in white, is simply stunning - Recommended

Tel; 0141 332 1263
web: www.15glasgow.com

Rates: £99.00-140 – varies from to room.

Somerset

Bath Lodge Castle - Norton St Philip, Bath – Somerset - BA2 7NH

If a hotel room simply won't do for the weekend, why not take a few pals with you and hire a castle?
Bath Lodge Castle is a unique boutique hotel in Bath, offering a romantic and informal 'castle experience'.

This Grade II listed fortress is bursting with character, and is complete, with towers, battlements and a portcullis. It is everything you would expect from a small castle and much more.

Located just six miles from Bath

Tel: 01225 723 043
web: www.clarenco.com/venues/bath-lodge-castle

Rates – see website.

Babington House – Babington near Frome Somerset
BA11 3RW United Kingdom

A two and a half hour drive from London or an hour and 20 minutes by train to Bath Spa, will bring you to the glorious county of Somerset, and the even more glorious Babington House.

All bedrooms are large, individually designed and equipped with the latest technology from Sony LCD screens and DVD players to wireless internet access. Most bathrooms have stand-alone baths, large showerheads and a selection of Cowshed bath products.

If you like your location a little more classic, and a little less hip, then this is the place for you.

There is a minimum two night stay per room from Friday to Saturday. From Sunday to Thursday, there is no minimum night stay.

Tel: 44 (0)1373 812266
web: www.babingtonhouse.co.uk

Rates - main house from £220.00

NB– because this is also a members club, it can get somewhat busy, make sure you book well in advance

The Queensberry Hotel - Russel Street, Bath - BA1 2QF

The Queensberry Hotel, is cetainly one of the most beautiful hotels in Bath. Run by the husband and wife team of Laurence & Helen Beere - the place has a very unique atmosphere.

True, there are larger hotels in this city, though I doubt there are many more lovely. This smart boutique hotel offers stylish accommodation and the attention to detail is evident. Each room is completely individual, so there is bound to be one that suits.

There is an in house restaurant - the Olive Tree - careful, you may never want to leave the hotel !

Tel: 44 (0)1225 447928
web www.thequeensberry.co.uk

Rates - from £99.00 see website

Dorian House - 1 Upper Oldfield Park, Bath BA2 3JX

This is one you really shouldn't miss. Set within a beautiful, period villa, a mere ten minute walk from the centre of Bath, Dorian House is really worth checking out.

The attention to detail is evident at every turn, from the marble bathrooms and pressure showers, to the Breakfast Orangery and the manicured gardens. This is the ideal base for touring this beautiful county, or simply chilling out in style.

Check out the website.

Tel +44(0)1225 426336
e mail info@dorianhouse.co.uk
web: www.dorianhouse.co.uk

Rates - £80 - £160

Features-
crisp cotton sheets
fluffy towels
tea/coffee making facilities
television

hairdryer & telephone

Suffolk

Tuddenham-Mill - High Street, Tuddenham, Nr. Newmarket, Suffolk - IP28 6SQ

This picturesque mill is situated on the Suffolk /Cambridgeshire border, so makes an ideal spot for discovering either county.

The bedrooms are delightful, a great mixture of old and contemporary. The addition of a top chef in-house, means your every whim can be catered for.

Tel: 44 (0)1638) 713552
web: www.tuddenhammill.co.uk

Rates – Mill Room from £185.00

Surrey

Bingham – 61-63 Petersham Road, Richmond Upon Thames, Surrey - TW10 6UT T

The property, originally built as two houses in 1740, was described in a rental survey for George III, carried out in 1773 as a "*messeuge* (a dwelling), court and garden" and a "*messuage* with stables and coach house".

This delightful riverside dwelling is now home to the Bingham, a luxurious boutique hotel and restaurant. No expense has been spared to create this haven by the Thames.

Great location for that weekend break or discovering London.

Tel: 44 (0) 20 8940 0902
web:

Rates: POA

Sussex

Black Rock House Hotel - 10 Stanley Road, Hastings,
East Sussex - TN34 1UE

This stylish boutique B&B set in a restored Victorian villa, has five individually designed, spacious guest-rooms, finished to an exacting standard. All rooms have contemporary en-suite facilities with; wet rooms, waterfall showers or full sized baths. Sumptuous beds dressed with Egyptian cotton, soft white towels, robes and luxury toiletries come as standard.

This small luxury hotel is a stone's throw from the beach, Hastings Station and the Old Town; so is ideally placed whether visiting for business or pleasure and includes complimentary parking for all guests.

Tel: 01424 438448
web: www.hastingsaccommodation.com/facilities.html

Rates - from £125.00

Sea Spray - 26 New Steine, Brighton - BN2 1PD

This boutique hotel offers a range of bedrooms, from superior stylish to suites with great sea views, fun themed doubles and swish penthouses

Sea Spray boutique hotel is also located on one of the best seafront squares, in central Brighton, and is just a short stroll from Brighton Beach, Brighton Pier and The Lanes - the premier shopping area of Brighton.

Tel : 44 (0)1273 680332
web: www.seaspraybrighton.co.uk

Rates – compact double from £60.00 weekdays.

Square - 4 New Steine, Brighton - BN2 1PB

An exclusive townhouse hotel and sophisticated bar located in fashionable Kemp Town, just off the seafront, in an immaculate regency garden square

Their ten rooms are decorated to the highest standard with designer fittings and striking en-suite bathrooms. All feature flat-screen TVs and DVD players and some have sea views.

Tel: 01273 691777
web: www.squarebrighton.com

Rates - Double room from £120.00

Check out website

Kemp Townhouse - 21 Atlingworth Street Brighton
BN2 1PL

Located in a beautiful listed building in the heart of
Kemp Town, Brighton, this Sophisticated boutique hotel
tick all the boxes.

A subtle blend of old-world elegance is mixed with
contemporary style and a healthy dose of English
eccentricity,

The rooms are relaxing and, oh so subtle. Convenient for
the Lanes, Brighton Pavilion and restaurants - great
reviews from press and public alike - this has to be the
best pitch in town !

Tel: 01273 681400
web: www.kemptownhousebrighton.com

Rates - small double from £95.00 weekdays. Check the
website for special deals.

Richmond House - 230 Oving Road, Chichester, West Sussex - PO19 7EJ

Looking for a great base from which to discover this beautiful county? Then look no further.

Richmond House is a boutique B&B that is sure to please. Situated a mere ten-minute walk from the centre of glorious Chichester, Richmond House offers complete style and comfort at a perfect price. The attention to detail is impressive, from the deep baths to the bespoke toiletries, here is a place that simply oozes quality.

Telephone: 01243 771464
web: www.richmondhousechichester.co.uk

Rate - from £70.00

Features -
free Wi Fi - iPod dock - TV with Freeview
Egyptian cotton bedding & towels
pocket sprung mattresses

Wales

Jolyons at No 10 - 10 Cathedral Road, Cardiff CF11 9LJ

This beautiful boutique hotel in the heart of Cardiff, is the last word in luxury. With 21 individually designed lavish rooms, finished to a superb standard, this hotel offers all you could want from your visit to this city.

All the rooms are beautifully furnished with fine furniture, thick upholstery and rich colour-tones for complete comfort. While the bathrooms at Jolyon's are just as luxurious and offer everything from extravagant plunge-pools (for two) to whirlpool jet baths and colour-light therapy.

Tel: +44 (0)2920 091 900
web: www.jolyons10.com

Rates - POA

St Brides Spa Hotel - St Brides Hill, Saundersfoot, Pembrokeshire - SA69 9NH

AA Hotel of the Year, Wales 2011 – 2012
Set on the beautiful Pembrokeshire coast, this stylish retreat off the perfect getaway weekend Most rooms have sea views and balcony. All are contemporary style, with a light and airy feel. Local touches have been introduced wherever possible through handmade furniture, woven bed throws and artwork.
So whether you want to walk cycle, swim or just chill out, this could be the perfect location.

Tel: 01834 812 304
Fax 01834 811 766
web: www.stbridesspahotel.com
e-mail: reservations@stbridesspahotel.com
or spa@stbridesspahotel.com

Features:
Free high speed Wi Fi
TV with Sky channels & radio stations
DVD player (We have a great selection of DVDs to cater for all tastes)
Tea & Coffee Making Facilities
Fridge
Safe
Comfort Zone products as used in our Marine Spa
Robes and Slippers
Hair dryer
Iron and board
Bath and shower

Rates - POA

Fronlas - Llandeilo, Carmarthenshire, Wales – SA19 6LB

Fronlas is a pretty, white Edwardian, boutique house-hotel, set in the town of Llandello (approx 25 miles north of Swansea).
There are just 4 double rooms at Fronlas, but don't let that put you off, for what this place lacks in size, it more than makes up for in décor and general style.

Each of the rooms is individually styled and all rooms feature unique wallpaper murals, organic mattresses, organic linen, towels and bathrobes, luxury en-suites, and toiletries by REN skincare, hot-drink making facilities, hair-dryer, flat-screen TVs with Freeview, DVD players, a work-area suitable for a laptop and free Wi-Fi access. In short, everything you could need for that special weekend.

Tel: 01558 824773
web: www.fronlas.co.uk

Rates – from £90.00 weekdays.
NB – you may strain to see some of the written detail on their website – shame.

Escape Boutique B&B - 48 Church Walks, Llandudno –
North Wales - LL30 2HL

Escape Llandudno prides itself on being the first and
original, contemporary boutique bed & breakfast hotel
in the area. Set in a delightful Victorian villa in this
popular North Wales resort, Escape offers 9 individually
designed rooms with features such as flat screen TVs,
Playstations and Wireless Broadband access.

Ideally situated for the many restaurants and
attractions this timeless resort has to offer.

If you like your hotels quirky and friendly, then this is
the place for you.

T: 01492 877776
F: 01492 878777
web: http://www.escapebandb.co.uk
e mail: info@escapebandb.co.uk

Rates – from £89.00

Manorhaus - Hill Street, Llangollen, Denbighshire - LL20 8EU

Manorhaus Llangollen is primarily a quality restaurant with the added bonus of 5 star boutique accommodation. Set within an historic Victorian townhouse in the heart of picturesque Llangollen, the hotel offers stylish modern guestrooms with all the 21st Century facilities you would expect.

There are six guestrooms, ranging from cosy doubles to a superior room with a private decked terrace, while four suites each have their own lounge and in-room bath. This is the perfect base for touring or simply relaxing in style.

Tel: 01978 860775
e mail:post@manorhaus.com
web: www.manorhausellangollen.com

Rates - from £115.00

The Outbuildings - Anglesey - Bodowyr Farm, Llangaffo, Anglesey, North Wales - LL60 6NH

With stunning views to Snowdonia and the mountains of the Lleyn Peninsula, North Wales, The Outbuildings is a glorious boutique B&B. The rooms are utterly delightful, and the atmosphere welcoming, so if you are looking for that retreat with a difference - look no further.

Tel 01248 430132
web: www.theoutbuildings.co.uk

Rates - from £85.00

Features
crisp Cologne and Cotton bedding
delicious soaps
TVs with Freeview
Bose radio and one with i pod dock
all rooms have king size beds, two with en suite bathroom's - two with en suite shower room's

Venetia - Lon Sarn Bach, Abersoch, Gwynedd - LL53 7EB

Welcome to Venetia, a beautiful Victorian Villa, sitting just minutes away from sheltered beaches and clear waters of Abersoch on the tip of the Llyn Peninsula, North Wales.

Best described as contemporary luxury. The Venetia boasts individually designed bedrooms with great attention to detail.

Perfectly placed for all that this delightful area offers - we recommend you linger on this website.

Tel: 44 (0)1758 713 354
web: www.venetiawales.com

Rates - from £98.00 (low season)

Features -
under floor heating
luxury Ginseng & Macadamia toiletries
powerful walk-in showers
Flare LED heated mirrors.
Flos lighting by Philippe Starck
floor to ceiling bespoke wardrobes
wall mounted LCD TVs
DVD player.

Warwickshire & West Midlands

Hampton Manor - Shadowbrook Lane,
Hampton-in-Arden, Solihull, West Midlands - B92 0EN

An independent hotel operated and developed by the Hill family. With over 20 years experience and the combination of operational experience and fresh vision, has combined to create the offering that stands today.

There are 12 individually designed rooms located in the original manor house, each fitted throughout with the Louis Collection of furniture by award winning designer John Reeves.

Tel:44 (0) 1675 446080
web: www.hamptonmanor.eu

Rates – POA

Wirral

Leverhulme Hotel – Port Sunlight Village, Wirral, Merseyside - CH62 5EZ

Set in the picturesque Garden Village of Port Sunlight on the Wirral peninsula, this grade 2-listed building has been lovingly converted into an art- deco styled boutique hotel. A mixture of classic 30s style and on-trend facilities, has lead to much acclaim since its restoration in 2008.

The building was originally opened in 1907 as a cottage hospital. It formed part of Lord Leverhulme's philanthropic scheme for Port Sunlight,

The Leverhulme boasts 19 stylish bedrooms, wine bar and restaurant.

Tel: 44 (0)151 644 6655
web: www.leverhulmehotel.co.uk

Rates - check out website

Features – based on 'Baby Grand' room
single seated area
hot beverages available on request
LCD TV with Playstation
2/DVD player
complimentary WIFI

Worcestershire

Eckington Manor - Hammock Road, Eckington, Worc's, WR10 3BJ

For a break with a difference this may just tick a few boxes. Your time at Eckington Manor can be spent exactly as you please, brushing up on your cookery skills, or simply relaxing in a bespoke bedroom

You may prefer however, to simply use the Manor as a base for touring this lovely county.

Tel: 01386 898679
web: www.eckingtonmanor-px.rtrk.co.uk

Rates – from £150.00 midweek.

Yorkshire

The Palm Court Hotel - St. Nicholas Cliff, Scarborough, North Yorkshire - YO11 2E

This hotel is a prime example of what is happening to this Yorkshire resort. A first- class hotel, that knows just what the discerning visitor is looking for, and knows how to provide the best.

Great position, and has the added advantage of having a quality restaurant as well. The perfect base to discover this spa town and the glorious countryside of North Yorkshire.

Tel: 01723 368161 |
web: www.palmcourt-scarborough.co.uk

Rates – executive suites from £140.00

42 The Calls – 42 The Calls, Leeds - LS2 7EW

This 18th Century former riverside corn mill has been converted into a stylish boutique hotel. Retaining many of its original features, it has been skilfully blended with a collection of original paintings and an eclectic mix of furnishing to create a very individual hotel.

This award winning hotel is homely and yet boutique, and has an honesty bar to allow guests an alternative place to meet and relax outside of their bedrooms. Complimentary Wi-Fi internet access.
Central Leeds Location

Tel: +44 (0)113 244 0099
web: www.42thecalls.co.uk

Rates – POA – there are a number of offers open.

Quebecs - 9 Quebec Street, Leeds, West Yorkshire - LS1 2HA

Built in 1891 as the "Leeds and County Liberal Club" one of the most distinctive terracotta brickwork buildings in Leeds.
This is now the home of Quebecs. If you like your hotels seriously luxurious and ultra classic, then this could be the one for you.

The rooms are simply sumptuous and as you would expect from a hotel of this calibre, fully equipped with - individually controlled air-conditioning, satellite LCD television, complimentary broadband, DDI telephone and voicemail, CD player, hairdryer, trouser press and ironing board, personal safe, complimentary magazines, a well stocked mini-bar, coffee and luxury tea making facilities.

Tel : 0113 244 8989
web: www.quebecshotel.co.uk

Rates: POA

The Balmoral Hotel – Franklin Mount, Harrogate, North Yorkshire - HG1 5EJ

The Balmoral Hotel has undergone an extensive refurbishment programme: everything from the foyer to the bar, to the suites themselves, has been re-vamped to a high standard. Combining the very best traditional elements and the best of confident contemporary style. The the result is a very impressive boutique hotel, perfectly situated to enjoy all this beautiful spa town has to offer.

The hotel has the added bonus of guest parking, friendly, professional service, and a great adjoining bar - Nice standard and good crit's

The facilities of the nearby Academy Spa, which is just a 5 minute drive from the hotel, are at your disposal. As hotel guests, you can enjoy complimentary use of the facilities as part of your stay, so you can work out in the fully-equipped gym, swim in the pool or relax in the lounge all free of charge

Tel: +44 (0) 1423 508208
web: balmoralhotel.co.uk
e-mail: info@balmoralhotel.co.uk

Executive rooms inc'
Double bed

Features –
en suite with shower or bath
tea and coffee making facilities with

plasma TV with Freeview
telephone
wireless internet in the lobby area
mineral water from Harrogate's very own spa
Molton Brown toiletries

Rates – POA
Check out the special weekend breaks

Boutique 25 - 25 Newmarket Street, Skipton, North Yorkshire- BD23 2JE

Set in the pretty market town of Skipton, this hotel would make the ideal location for discovering the beautiful Yorkshire Dales.

There are 5 very individually designed guestrooms - that range from French Boudouir to Urban Chic. Whatever your preference, you can be assured that boutique offers a high standard of comfort and service

Tel: 01756 79 36 76
web: www.boutique25.co.uk

Rates - from £99.00 - see website

Features
Dependant upon room
king size bed
roll top bath
CD player & mini bar

The Bijou - 17 Ripon Road, Harrogate - HG1 2JL

This privately owned and managed hotel is set within a Victorian villa in the fashionable neighbourhood of Harrogate's Duchy Estate.

There are 10 individually designed guestrooms, all en – suite, and all featuring the full facilities you would expect from such a hotel. This is the perfect location for discovering this beautiful county, or simply just chilling out in comfort.

Tel: 44 (0)1423 567974
Fax: 01423 566200
web: www.thebijou.co.uk

Rates - POA

Features -
flat screen LCD television
crisp white linen and mellow soft furnishings
en-suite tiled bathrooms

hospitality tray with fairtrade coffee/tea & biscuits a
hairdryer, Radio/Alarm clock
DVD player available on request
luxury Cole and Lewis toiletries

waffle bathrobes

The Grafton - 1–3 Franklin Mount, Harrogate, North Yorkshire - HG1 5EJ

This elegant boutique hotel is a short walk from all that Harrogate has to offer. The hotel has 14 stunning, ultra - stylish guestrooms, all en-suite, and all simply outstanding in quality and design.

In the owner's words - 'Whether visiting for business or pleasure The Grafton is the perfect place to make your base, combining a homely atmosphere with contempor - ary, stylish surroundings. It's ideal for those who want the sophistication of a large hotel without sacrificing personal service and attention to detail.'

We couldn't agree more -
Check out the website !

Tel: 01423 508491
web: www.graftonhotel.co.uk

Rates - from £90.00

The Marine Hotel - 13 Marine Parade, Whitby, North Yorkshire - YO21 3PR

The sister hotel to the Moon & Sixpence. The Marine is again ideally situate for all that Whitby has to offer. The hotel offers four delightful guestrooms , and again the attention to detail is evident, as is the quality throughout.

From the roll top baths or quality showers to the fluffy towels, the care for the gust is obvious. The views are free !

Tel: 44 (0)1947 605022
web: www.the-marine-hotel.co.uk

Rates - POA

Features
LCD TV
king size beds
en-suite bath or shower
room service

Yorebridge House - Bainbridge, North Yorkshire Dales, DL8 3EE

Situated by the river on the edge of the unspoilt village of Bainbridge, Wensleydale in the North Yorkshire Dales, the Yorebridge provides the ideal base for discovering The Dales.

The hotel offers an impressive selection of stylish rooms , each individual, each offering an exceptional standard of luxury and comfort.- this is a boutique hotel in every sense of the word.

There are slipper baths, wet room showers and so much more - take a close look at the website.

Tel: 01969 652060
web: www.yorbridgehouse.co.uk

Rates - from £190.00 - see website

The Ultimate Names

London

Browns - Albemarle Street, London - W1S 4BP

Brown's Hotel is a luxury 5-star hotel in London central. This famous hotel first opened its doors for business in 1837, and has been going strong ever since.

Acquired by the Rocco Forte Group in 2003. this sedate building set in the heart of Mayfair on Albermarle Street offers the perfect, low key, quality accommodation for your London stay. .

Universally recognised as one of the finest of its type in the world, it's perfectly located for all of London's top attractions, and is within easy walking distance of Bond Street, Regent Street and theatre-land.

It also sits on the doorstep of Green Park and Hyde Park.

Tel:44(0)20 7493 6020
web: www.brownshotel.com

Rates – POA

Claridges -49 Brook Street City of Westminster, London
W1K 4HR

Famous for afternoon tea and much more, Claridges was founded in 1812 as Mivart's Hotel. Located in a conventional London terrace, it grew by expanding into several neighbouring properties, until 1854, when the founder sold the hotel to a Mr and Mrs Claridge, who owned a smaller hotel next door.

They combined the two operations, and after trading for a time as "Mivart's at Claridge's", they settled on the current name.

Such is the worldwide reputation of this grand hotel, with its stunning Art Deco interior and immaculate service, that it would be easier to say which famous person hasn't visited the iconic establishment.

Whether you are looking to spend a romantic week or weekend in London, or you simply want to experience afternoon tea in its sumptuous surroundings – there is no finer place to visit or stay.

Tel; 44(0)20 7107 8860
web: www.claridges.co.uk

Rates - POA

The Dorchester - Park Lane, London - W1K 1QA

Once again this iconic hotel on Park Lane, in Mayfair needs no introduction. The High 30s style exterior is famous throughout the world, and has been a firm favourite of stars and politicians for decades.

Despite its outward appearance, the Dorchester is a grand hotel in the classic style, not stylized modern.

With views over Hyde Park, and its central position midway between the West-End and Knighstbridge, makes it the ideal London location.

Telephone: +44 (0) 20 762988
web: www.thedorchester.com

Rates – POA

Hotel 41 – 41 Buckingham Palace Road, London - SW1W 0PS

It's appropriate that this hotel has such an address, because the service here is akin to being treated like a Royal.

This most traditional of hotels has a lively, almost quirky interior, part classic, part contemporary. If you are looking for a 5star hotel in a great location, you can do no better.

Check out the various reviews, we think you'll like this one.

Tel: 44(0)207 3000041
web: www.41hotel.com

Rates – POA

The Ritz -The Ritz London, 150 Piccadilly, London, United Kingdom W1J 9BR

This 5 star hotel is so famous, that Noel Coward actually included it in one of his songs - 'A Nightingale Sang in Berkeley Square', and is generally recognized as the basis for the show tune 'Putting on The Ritz'.

A firm favourite of Royals and commoners alike, this is a very special hotel. The Ritz's most famous facility is the Palm Court, a masterpiece in over the top, cream-colored Louis XVI styling.

This is the venue for the world-famous institution that is now simply referred to as "Tea at the-Ritz.

Great central location, here you are right at the heart of the West-End.

Tel: 020 7493 8181
web: www.theritzlondon.com

Rates – POA

The Savoy –Strand, City of London, London - WC2R 0EU

The Savoy is one of the grandest of the London hotels, and has recently undergone an extensive and meticulous re-styling (costing an eye watering £220 million).

The famous fusion of Art Deco and Edwardian style has been retained and embellished, with 268 rooms and suites, offering every comfort and modern convenience to the discerning traveller, this is a must stay hotel.

The list of famous visitors to pass through this most iconic of entrances is huge and impressive. Close to the best that the West–End has to offer, its unique position bordering the River Thames, adds that extra something special to an evening in London.

Tel; 020 7836 4343
web: www.fairmont.com/savoy-london

Rates – POA

Outside London

Cliveden House – Taplow , Berkshire - SL6 0JF

The former home of The Astor family, Cliveden House became a country house hotel in 1984.
The 38 Bedrooms and suites + cottage are set within the heart of the glorious Berkshire countryside. Surrounded by 376 acres of magnificent National Trust managed Grade I listed formal gardens and parkland, Cliveden offers fabulous panoramic views over the River Thames.

Very often the term luxury hotel can be an overblown statement of the actual facts, not in the case of Cliveden, this is true luxury on a grand scale.
With easy access to Heathrow Airport and good road networks, this has to be a great choice for that out of London experience.

I believe you can also book for afternoon tea as a non-resident – check out their extensive website.

Tel: 00 44 1628 668561
web: www.clivedenhouse.co.uk

Rates – POA

The Midland - 16 Peter St, Manchester - M60 2D

Like so many original Railway hotels, this is a huge place. The Midland was considered at one time to be one of the finest hotels outside of London.

This 4-star luxury hotel is situated right in the heart of Manchester, so is ideal for concerts theatres and restaurants. It has stylish, air-conditioned rooms with free Wi-Fi, and a pool, gym and squash court. The French Restaurant has won 2 AA Rosettes.

If you are a history buff, you may be interested to know that, this is the place where Charles Rolls met Henry Royce in 1904, and the rest, as they say – is history
This is the ideal location for you business or weekend break.

Tel: 44 (0)161 236 3333
web: www.qhotels.co.uk

Rates POA

Stapleford Park - Stapleford, Nr. Melton Mowbray, Leicestershire - LE14 2EF

If you are looking for the grandest of weekends, then it would be hard to imagine a more sublime setting than Stapleford Park.

This magnificent country house is set in 500 acres of landscaped grounds – and offers the perfect luxury hotel and English sporting country retreat.

Set in rural Leceistershire near Melton Mowbray, and just minutes from the beautiful Rutland Water. This hotel is simply sublime.

Overnight guests can choose from 55 individually designed bedrooms – when they say individual rooms, that is exactly what they mean – you really must do your homework on this one, so as to ensure you are booking the room of your preference.

Tel: +44 (0) 1572 787000
web: www.staplefordpark.com

Rates – house rooms from £288.00

Gleneagles - Auchterarder, Auchterarder, Scotland - PH3 1BR -

If you like you retreat hotel to be in a sublime location, serving fine wines and food. If you want to stay in a Chateau-style hotel set in rolling glens, and take in the odd game of golf - then look no further.

Gleneagles is all these things and so much more, built by the former Caledonian Railway Company, with its own railway station.

The Gleneagles Hotel is now owned by Diageo plc, and from the reception areas to the classic-rooms, the whole place shouts luxury and service.

Freephone: 0800 389 3737 (UK only)
web: www.gleneagles.com
Rates - POA

The Fairmont – St Andrews , Scotland - KY16 8PN

Set within a 520 acre estate in the unique coastal setting of St Andrews, the home of Golf and university fame , this stunning hotel is the perfect destination for that escape holiday or celebrating that family occasion.

From lavish bedrooms to a luxurious spa, world class golf to exquisite dining, this hotel has it all.

The Fairmont guestrooms have an option of king or twin room – the twin boasts two queen size beds for ultimate comfort.

The Spa's luxurious 12 treatment rooms offer a range of treatments which include locally-themed massages, facial and relaxation therapies featuring exclusive Kerstin Florian and Pure Lochside products

Tel: 44 1334 837000
Fax: 44 1334 837099
web: www.fairmont.com

Suggestions

If you have any suggestions for your favourite luxury or boutique hotel, then why not let us know.
Simply attach the name and website address, and e mail it to -
info@bookopedia.co.uk

Thank you

Thanks

A huge thank you to the following people for their tireless efforts and general good advice in compiling this guide.

Georgina Heald
John Brown
David Carlyle

For hotels, offers and travel links - why not visit our website at -

www.brownsguide.co.uk

Disclaimer

All Reasonable care has been taken to ensure that the information presented in this book is accurate. However, the reader should understand that the information provided does not constitute legal, or professional advice of any kind. .

No Liability:

This product is supplied "as is" and without warranties. All warranties, express or implied, are hereby disclaimed. Use of this product constitutes acceptance of the "No Liability" policy

The author or Bookopedia shall not be liable for any losses or damages whatsoever(including, without limitation, consequential loss or damage) directly or indirectly arising from the use of this product.

Printed in Great Britain
by Amazon